Paganism:

A Religion for the 21st Century

by
Shanddaramon

Paganism:

A Religion for the 21st Century

Paganism
A Religion for the 21ˢᵗ Century
by Shanddaramon

First Edition (Softcover)
Published by:
Astor Press
http://www.astorpress.com

ΛST⊕R
[PRESS]

ISBN: 978-0-578-01799-0

Produced in the United States of America

The author may be contacted at mail@shanddaramon.com.
For more information visit http://www.shanddaramon.com.

Table of Contents

Prelude

"*The most beautiful experience we can have is the mysterious. It is the fundamental emotion which stands at the cradle of true art and true science.*" ~ *Einstein*

uesday morning. The handsome looking middle-aged couple I see come into this coffee shop every time I am in it are here again. They exchange some giggles and some comments about the current political climate and then proceed to head to the counter to order their usual caffeinated drinks. As they get in line, they pass by a host of people on their laptops who are usually checking their e-mail. I am one of those people at a laptop tapping away at a small table. They do not know my name but they wave cheerfully because that's what people who are regulars at a particular coffee shop do. This time, however, in the hopes of starting an interesting conversation, they ask me what it is that I am working on so diligently.

I am often a little reluctant to discuss my writing with people I do not know. When someone asks me what I am doing, I feel compelled to be honest in my answer to them but I also tend to be coy. I usually just tell them I am writing. Some push on and ask what it is I am writing. When I say I am writing about religion sometimes people suddenly become alarmed. They assume I am writing about one particular religion because, in our culture, the word religion is often linked specifically to Christianity and they are afraid that, if they continue to talk to me, I will eventually try to convert them. It is at that point that they will kindly excuse themselves and move away.

If I say I am writing about spirituality, some will feel less threatened and may continue to ask me more questions. When I say I am writing about Paganism then an even more alarming look may subtly cross their face. They may move along quickly for fear that I may vex them with some evil curse. On even more rare occasions, I will run into a fellow Pagan who will ask about some more specifics concerning my writing and we might even have a short discussion. This, however, is usually not the case. To avoid all the hassle and confusion I usually just tell people I am checking my email.

Sometimes, though, there comes along a person who is simply curious and wants to learn more. This person often just wants to know some basic information about Paganism. She or he may find that contemporary culture and the traditional religions seem to be in conflict. Because of this, that person may be open to new spiritual possibilities and ideas. Often, this person is not content with just getting by every day and searches for deep meaning and a purpose to life that has not been found in the teaching of the religion of his or her birth. He or she may be quite independent in thinking and living and is concerned with how we treat one another. It is for this person that I was inspired to write this book. In it are the answers to the most common questions people have about Paganism: what is it, is it really a religion, is it relevant to our lives, and what does it mean to be one?

Introduction

"Born again? No, I am not. Excuse me for getting it right the first time." ~
Dennis Miller

My Goals For This Book

odern Paganism is spreading throughout the world and has been listed as one of the fastest growing modern religious movements yet it also one of the most misunderstood. It is my hope that books like this one will help dispel some of the confusion about this movement. I do this not just because I think my religion is the only right one and that I think everyone else should believe as I do - not at all. I do not believe that any one religion is the only correct one for all of humankind but I do think that the challenges and troubles of our world and our times require a new way of thinking and a new way of acting toward each other, toward ourselves, and toward the planet upon which we live. The way to make changes for the better, however, is to first make a change in our attitudes and in how we view the world. One of the ways to do this is through a religious perspective and I believe that modern Paganism offers a perspective that is right for our current times and conditions.

This book is for different people. There may be some who are interested in Paganism as a personal religion but who are unsure or unclear about it. There may be others who are not interested in becoming Pagan but want to know more about Pagan theories about life and living. There may be those who have some misconceptions about Paganism and who want to understand the truth and there may be those who are simply curious about the role of Paganism in the landscape of modern religious movements. Each person should be able to find something here to satisfy their needs.

This book is not an introduction to Paganism. There are already several great texts available for that purpose. My goals for this text are somewhat different than those usually reserved for introductory books. I wish to examine the role of Paganism within the context of modern religious and social needs and conditions. Specifically, I have three goals for this work: 1) to demonstrate that modern Paganism is a truly a religion, 2) to dispel some of the fears and misconceptions about the tenets and practices of Paganism, and (3) to demonstrate that modern Paganism is a religion that is suited and needed for the conditions and challenges of our lives in the 21st century.

Use of the Term Pagan

Throughout this book I will be discussing a modern religious movement that I identify by using the word Paganism. Unfortunately, this word is fraught with difficulties. First of all, the word pagan (small letter "p") has been traditionally used to refer to any number of different religious traditions considered pre-Christian or, sometimes, non-Christian. Starting in the middle of the 20th Century, a religious movement began to emerge whose adherents looked back to some of these pre-Christian Earth-based and nature based practices for inspiration. They called themselves Wiccans, Witches, Druids, Shamans, Asatru, and many other names but many recognized that they shared some similar convictions. The umbrella term Pagan was used when referring to any of these or similar movements. In reality, no one knows for sure what many of the ancient pagans believed or practiced since few things were written down and much of what was recorded was systematically destroyed or eradicated. Though modern Pagans may look back in time for inspiration, what they have developed is really a new religious movement. As Isaac Bonewits has pointed out, the true term for all these modern movements is Neopaganism. The prefix "neo" means recent or new but often refers to some tradition in the past. I prefer to use the simpler term Paganism (with a capital P) to refer to these new movements.

Misconceptions

Before we begin to look at Paganism as a serious and important religion for our times, let us first be clear on what Paganism is not. Paganism is often quickly dismissed when it comes up in conversations partially because of the connotations historically attached to the word and partially because so little is understood of this new movement. So many images have been created and passed on depicting Pagans as evil, self-centered, and immoral that it is often difficult to ask people to be open minded when discussing Paganism as a serious movement. When conversation is struck, some people often look for confirmations of their pre-determined opinions. Let us take one example. Some Pagans are polytheistic (some are also monotheistic and some are atheistic). There is a prevailing attitude that religious history has proceeded from polytheism to monotheism because such a progression demonstrates a maturity in human theological development. In a curious contradiction, some religious authorities who deny the concept of evolution consider the move from polytheism to monotheism to be our natural theological evolution. Pagans, then, are seen as regressive and ignorant of the obvious superiority of monotheism. If we were to follow this logic, however, we would have to accept atheism as the next and greater religious perspective. In reality, there is nothing (other than personal faith) that proves that one view is more correct than another.

Another reason that Paganism is dismissed is because it is seen by some as a spirituality only for social misfits. It is true that some Pagans like to wear all dark clothing, play Dungeons and Dragons late into the night, and wear pentagrams the size of hubcaps (and there is nothing wrong with any of that) but these folks do not represent the vast majority of Pagans. There are Pagans everywhere; they live in every state and every city. There are Pagans in many countries throughout the world and they work in a variety of places. There are Pagan lawyers, doctors, professors, teachers, and professionals in all areas of work and there are Pagans who fix cars and run stores and restaurants. In my favorite local coffee shop where I often go to write, one of the servers is openly Pagan. In other words, there are Pagans in every type of living, working, and social situation.

A third reason that Pagans are often dismissed is because people believe that they mean to be harmful. They point to the common and incorrect traditional view of Pagans as devil worshippers who practice various forms of sacrifice and spew hateful incantations. Though there are some who honor Satan as a deity of chaos and transformation (and there is a great deal of debate by

Pagans as to whether those people should be considered Pagans) none that I know of worship a concept of evil known as the devil. Instead, many Pagans vow to "harm none" and focus their energies on healing the earth and the beings who live there.

In short, Paganism is a modern theological movement whose adherents, like those of any major religion, are normal every day people from all walks of life. But, is Paganism really a religion like Christianity or Islam or is it a passing fad like the hula hoop? It turns out that such a simple question is really quite difficult to answer.

Chapter One

Paganism as a Religion

"Religion consists in a set of things which the average man thinks he believes and wishes he was certain of." –Mark Twain

Introduction

In this chapter I wish to tackle the question of whether modern Paganism can be considered a spirituality, a religion, or just a curious fad. To do this, we will need to understand what is meant by the term Paganism, determine a definition for spirituality and religion, and then see if Paganism fits into either or both of these definitions. I realize that by even taking on this venture that I am entering into stormy seas. The word religion can have a variety of connotations. People tend to define the word by the religious practice they know or were brought up upon. If a person's past experience with a particular religion was oppressive or even abusive then those associations will be carried on into anything that may be defined as a religion. We need, then, to define religion by the qualities of more than a single religious tradition. Those who see religion in negative terms may then turn to spirituality and may reject anything they practice as being a religion. Can a spirituality also be a religion? To answer this, we will need a definition of spirituality and an understanding of how spirituality relates to religion.

What Is Paganism?

I mentioned that this book would not be an introductory text on Paganism but we do need to understand what is meant by the use of the term itself. Defining Paganism is actually more difficult than defining many of the traditional religions. That is because the traditional religions have common creeds by which all their practitioners are expected to accept and live. This is not the case for Paganism. There is no set doctrine or required creed that all Pagans must accept. I believe that is one of the strengths of Paganism but it can make it difficult to take on a study such as the one I have initiated here. If there is no clear definition of Paganism, then we cannot determine if it meets any other definitions. Clearly, most Pagans set themselves apart from the traditional religious traditions. Something, then, must make them different. Modern Pagans are often fiercely independent and, for reasons listed above and others, many do not like to define their practice as a religion nor do they like to seek a common set of principles. I believe, however, that even though there are several different flavors of Paganism, there are still some defining principles. It is like making ice cream, if you will. The core of ice cream consists of sugar, and cream. These are solidified through the use of ice and rock salt. From these basic ingredients can be added different flavorings such as vanilla, chocolate, or strawberries. Thus, there are different flavors of ice cream but they all share the same basic ingredients. The same is true for Paganism. I believe that there are three primary ingredients to all the different flavors of Paganism and I call these basic principles the Three Pillars of Paganism.

The Three Pillars of Paganism

1) The sacred exists within and beyond all things making all things and creatures sacred.
2) Because of our inherent sacredness, we are free to make our own spiritual and life choices but we know that we are ultimately responsible for the consequences of those choices.
3) All things exist in cycles and we celebrate and honor those cycles both personally and communally.

I call these Three Pillars: Sources, Choices, and Cycles. I believe that if you look at the statements of faith of many of the Pagan groups out there that you will find variations on these three basic themes. How each group celebrates the divine and what specific choices they make for honoring it are the ways in which the many flavors of Paganism are added.

This first Pillar implies both a dissolving and resolving of the divine. Let us look first at the dissolution. Imagine a glass of water and a piece of rock salt. If you put the rock salt in the water and stirred up the glass, it would eventually dissolve in the water to the point where it might even seem to disappear. If you put a string back into the glass and let it stay there for some time the salt would begin to form crystals on the string and reappear. The first Pillar states that all of creation, all creatures, and all people everywhere are equally part of the sacredness of the universe. All things are sacred because they all possess the same divine essence. (I prefer to use the term "Spirit" and will do so throughout the book but feel free to substitute your own favorite word for the divine.) Pagans are often called Earth-Centered because most believe that the Earth is a living organism that should be honored and respected as our Mother Earth. For many Pagans, Spirit exists within all things and is the essence of all things. They accept the notion put forth by Albert Einstein expressed in the formula $E = MC^2$ where E is energy, M is mass, and C is what Einstein believed to be the only universal constant: the speed of light (186,000 miles per second). The formula means that all mass is simply slower vibrations of energy; the whole universe is energy. Thus, all things contain the same essence - which is energy - but even Einstein said that he believed there was something behind the energy that brought the universe together. That brings us to the resolution part of the formula.

Many Pagans believe that there is a single underlying source to all of the universe to which all things return. This source can be the same energy source that is within all things. Water, for example, can exist as separate raindrops or particles of mist but is still essentially water and all raindrops and mist eventually return to larger bodies of water. The flow of one form of water into another creates endless cycles of change and renewal. Like the salt crystals that disappear into the water and appear invisible, all beings and things eventually return to the divine source. When I speak of divinity here I am not necessarily referring to a sacred being or god (or goddess for that matter). Some Pagans believe in gods, usually as part of an ancient or created pantheon, while others do not. Some speak of God and Goddess not as anthropomorphic entities but as metaphors to represent the natural forces of masculine and feminine (or yin and yang). Others make no mention of deities but honor Nature, Earth, Spirit, the Higher Self, or Energy as the ultimate reality of the universe. One of the unique things about Paganism is that you are free to determine this ultimate reality for yourself. This brings us to the second Pillar.

The second Pillar states that Pagans are free to define for themselves what is both within and beyond all things and that they are free to choose how to honor and celebrate that understanding. This principle is different than what many of the world's major religions expect of their adherents. Most major religions maintain a specific creed or set of principles to which all practitioners are expected to obey. For many Western religions, there is a god that expects obedience to the rules but, with Paganism, there is no deity who requires no such obedience. Pagans have a wide variety of views on divinity but still call themselves Pagan even if they disagree on their understanding of the details. In some other religions, such disagreements would require that people with different ideas would have to break off from the main church and begin their own sect. When a religion sets out a specific doctrine, it then also claims that its doctrine is the only correct and true one and that all others are false.

This, of course, leads to theological debates and sometimes even deadly conflicts. Paganism avoids much (but not all) of this when its adherents agree to tolerate each other's different views. Many Pagans extend this tolerance toward the practitioners of all other religions besides just their own.

The second part of the second Pillar reminds Pagans that they are responsible for the choices they make. That is because we know the sacred is within each of us. We cannot blame a deity or other power for forcing us to take the actions we choose to take. Each person is responsible for what he or she believes and for the decisions that he she makes based on that world view. This means that both ethical and spiritual choices need to be made by each individual Pagan. No one can give us the answers; we must find them on our own. Thus, each Pagan must go through his or her own personal quest to find ways in which to believe, worship, and act in the world. Furthermore, Pagans know they are responsible not only for their decisions but for the consequences produced as a result of the actions based on those decisions. We cannot claim that a sacred book or a voice from a god directed us to cause harm to another nor can we use others to justify our actions. Pagans are open to constantly learning and refining their ideas rather than setting them in stone for all eternity. We understand that all people change and this brings us to the third Pillar.

The third Pillar requires us to think about the universe in a different way than has traditionally been done before. Western culture tends to think in terms of straight lines: things have a beginning, a middle, and an end, and that is it! A straight line also makes clear distinctions between any two objects or choices; everything must be one thing or the other. Pagans look to Nature to learn about life and how to live together. There is no need for a sacred text because everything that needs to be learned can be sought out through Nature. When you observe the natural world you will come to learn at least one important principle: Nature knows no straight lines. Even lines that seem straight like the horizon are just an illusion. Nothing in Nature is ever completely one thing or another. All things have some element of their opposite within them. We can learn much about our own lives from this principle. One way that these constant cycles can be readily observed is by observing and honoring the movements of the celestial bodies around us.

Pagans look to the cycles of the moon and the sun to teach them about the cycles of life. Life is not just a birth-life-death straight line, it is part of the many cycles of life and death. All energy manifests into form and then returns to another form of energy. Spirit lives and dances through all of its temporary manifestations. One of the most important cycles for all of us is the constant change of seasons. They affect all of us regardless of philosophy, culture, shape, or form. Even though we have gone to great extremes to separate ourselves from Nature, we cannot escape her. We dress, act, live, and interact differently in Winter than we do in Summer (especially if you live in a place like Massachusetts like I do). Pagans honor the days that mark the changes in the seasons. The Winter and Summer Solstice and the Spring and Fall Equinoxes are considered sacred days. Four other days between those days are also considered sacred as they mark the height of the seasons.

Paganism does not require that people come together to celebrate their faith. Some Pagans are strictly solitary. They practice privately at home in their own way and do not feel a need to join with others in a spiritual community. The absolute solitary is rare, however, and most Pagans enjoy some amount of sharing with a community of like-minded people or with understanding friends. Some community is found in social circles or on the internet through chat channels and email lists. Others like to join together in groups and celebrate through specific rituals that honor the change in the seasons or other events in the lives of the participants.

Some Pagan Practices

1) Meditation
2) Prayer (sometimes practiced as spell work or magick)
3) Ritual celebrations of seasonal and life events and various rituals associated with degree training

---

So, there they are: the Three Pillars of Paganism. These shall be the principles by which I will define the modern movement of

Paganism and determine how Paganism might fit into the religious landscape of the 21st century. If you agree with them then you can follow along with the rest of my arguments. If you disagree with them (and I respect your freedom to do so) then you may need to suspend your disagreement so that you may continue to follow along with me (if you so desire).

What Is A Religion?

To determine if Paganism is a religion or a spirituality we must first define what a religion is (and, subsequently, what a spirituality is as well). Defining what the term religion means turns out to be equally, if not more, difficult than defining Paganism because there are so many varied definitions. Let us begin with some dictionary definitions. I will number each definition so that we may refer to them later.

I. Dictionary Definitions

I.a "..no single definition will suffice to encompass the varied sets of traditions, practices, and ideas which constitute different religions." (Barnes and Noble (Cambridge) Encyclopedia)

I.b. "Human recognition of superhuman controlling power and especially of a personal God entitled to obedience." (Concise Oxford Dictionary)

I.c. "A cause, principle, or system of beliefs held to with ardor and faith." (Merriam-Webster's Online Dictionary)

I.d. "Any specific system of belief and worship, often involving a code of ethics and a philosophy." (Webster's New World Dictionary)

I.e. "All concepts concerning the belief in god(s) and goddess(es) as well as other spiritual beings or transcendental ultimate concerns." (Penguin Dictionary of Religions)

I.f. "Human beings' relation to that which they regard as holy, sacred, spiritual, or divine." (Encyclopædia Britannica)

I.g. "A religion is a set of beliefs and practices, often centered upon specific supernatural and moral claims about reality, the cosmos, and human nature, and often codified as prayer, ritual, and religious law. " (Wikipedia)

Next, we will look at some definitions by philosophers.

II. Definitions by Philosophers

II.a "Religion is (subjectively regarded) the recognition of all duties as divine commands." (Immanuel Kant)

II.b. "[Religion is] our life's instinctive leap toward its origin, the motion by which we acknowledge the order and harmony to which we belong." (Wendell Berry)

II.c. "Religion originates in an attempt to represent and order beliefs, feelings, imaginings and actions that arise in response to direct experience of the sacred and the spiritual. (Paul Connelly)

II.d. "Religion is being ultimately concerned about that which is and should be our ultimate concern." (Paul Tillich)

II.e. "[Religion is] whatever introduces genuine perspective." (Dewey)

II.f. "[Religion is] the belief that there is an unseen order, and that our supreme good lies in harmoniously adjusting ourselves thereto." (William James)

II.g. "[Religion is] the knowledge possessed by the finite mind of its nature as absolute mind." (George Hegel)

II.h. "Religion is what the individual does with his own solitariness." (Alfred North Whitehead)

II.i. "A religion is a unified system of beliefs and practices relative to sacred things, that is to say, things set apart and forbidden." (Emile Durkheim)

II.j. "[A] religion is: a system of symbols which acts to establish powerful, pervasive and long-lasting moods and motivations in men by formulating conceptions of a general order of existence and clothing these conceptions with such an aura of factuality that the moods and motivations seem uniquely realistic." (Clifford Geertz)

Here are some definitions by authors:

III. Definitions by Authors

III.a. "The sacred is just the presence felt in the silence during the moment of genuine awareness." (Albert Camus)

III.b. "[Religion is] a compilation of suggestions and techniques by which we might become receptive to the supernatural and encourage or discourage its operation in our lives." (Michael York)

III.c. "[Religion is] to know that what is impenetrable to us really exists [and which] our dull faculties can comprehend only in their most primitive form - this knowledge, this feeling, is at the center of true religiousness." (Albert Einstein)

III. d "Religion is to do right. It is to love, it is to serve, it is to think, it is to be humble." (Ralph Waldo Emerson)

Finally, here are some definitions from the authors of web pages that deal with religion:

IV. Definitions by Websites

IV.a. "Religions are bodies of doctrine that specify a way of life centered on the maximization of the good, where the good includes both morality and right purpose." (progressiveliving.org)

IV.b. "Religion is any specific system of belief about deity, often involving rituals, a code of ethics, a philosophy of life, and a worldview. (A worldview is a set of basic, foundational beliefs concerning deity, humanity and the rest of the universe.)" (religioustolerance.org)

IV.c. "[Religion is defined as having:]
- A belief in something sacred.
- A distinction between sacred and profane objects.
- Ritual acts focused on sacred objects.
- A moral code believed to have a sacred or supernatural basis.
- Characteristically religious feelings, which tend to be aroused in the presence of sacred objects and during the practice of ritual.
- Prayer and other forms of communication with the supernatural.
- A world view, or a general picture of the world as a whole and the place of the individual therein. This picture contains some specification of an over-all purpose or point of the world and an indication of how the individual fits into it.
- A more or less total organization of one's life based on the world view.
- A social group bound together by the above."
(Austin Cline from About.com)

Finding A Good Definition

As you can see, there are quite a number of definitions on religion and they can be all be quite different from each other. I have only listed a few here but I think they represent a good spectrum of ideas. We will need to find a good working definition of religion first before we can determine if Paganism meets that definition. The easy thing to do, of course, would be to simply pick a definition that appears to work well for Paganism and call it a day. I would like to take a more careful approach, however. We will look at some possible limiting factors for the definitions above and keep a scorecard of which ones are being eliminated as we go. Here is what the scorecard will look like:

I.a	I.b.	I.c.	I.d.	I.e.	I.f.	I.g.			
II.a.	II.b.	II.c.	II.d.	II.e.	IIf.	IIg.	II.h.	II.i.	II.j.
III.a.	III.b.	III.c.	III.d.						
IV.a.	IV.b.	IV.c.							

In order to find a good workable definition of religion we will begin by creating three main parameters: 1) the definition should not be too narrow, 2) the definition should not be too vague, and 3) the definition should be simple and direct in helping us to define a particular practice as a religion.

A narrow definition would focus solely on one religion while disregarding the possibility of conflicting ideas. This was the case with earlier definitions that used only one single practice as the standard for defining religion in general. Definition I.b. speaks of a personal God who expects obedience. Clearly, this is a reference to the god recognized in Christianity and, to some degree, to the other Abrahamic religions but does not reflect the attitudes of other, especially Eastern, religions. Definition I.e. claims that all religions must include a belief in "spiritual beings" which assumes that such beings must exist. Definition II.g. uses the term "absolute mind" which seems to me to require the presence of an absolute being to possess this great mind which then leads us into the same difficulty as the other two definitions already mentioned. Definition II.i. seems to be fine until we get to the word *forbidden*. For something to be considered forbidden, there must be a ruling deity to decide what is and is not acceptable. Such a god is found in the Abrahamic religions but not in others. IV.b. also uses the term deity (though on their website they do say that even those who dismiss the concept of a deity are still forming a belief about deity). Even though this may seem to be a more open kind of definition, it still requires that all religions must form a concept of deity. If we are going to be open enough to accept Buddhism, Atheism, Humanism, and some other theologies as worthy of falling under a comprehensive definition of religion then we must not allow the concept of a deity to be the primary factor in such a definition. A good definition must be inclusive. With those thoughts in mind we can now darken out some of the definitions in our scorecard:

I.a.	I.b.	I.c.	I.d.	I.e.	I.f.	I.g.			
II.a.	II.b.	II.c.	II.d.	II.e.	II.f.	II.g.	II.h.	II.i.	II.j.
III.a.	III.b.	III.c.	III.d.						
IV.a.	IV.b.	IV.c.							

The pitfall of seeking inclusiveness in a good definition of religion, however, is to run to the other extreme and be too vague. A definition can be too vague in two ways: it can claim that there can be no good definition of religion or it can claim that anything can be a religion. Either method does not help us to find a clear definition of the word. Definition I.a. leans to the former fault of vague definitions by claiming that there can be no such clear understanding of the word at all. On the other end of the spectrum, number I.f. says that anything that someone thinks is holy or spiritual is their religion. Through this explanation, I could claim that fishing is my religion. I can say that when I go fishing that it is the most sacred activity that I know. This is not to say that going fishing cannot possibly be a spiritual event. Any activity can be sacred but it is not the activity itself that makes something a religious experience, it is the attitude and state of being that is obtained within and beyond that activity. It is my belief that the sacred and the religious must deal with our understanding of that which is greater than the self. Granted, this is my own bias, but it is a basic premise of all the major religions in the world and I think it is a good basis for limiting the the definitions of religion. If you accept this premise as well then we can agree that an activity that focuses solely on the fulfillment of the desires of the ego is not sacred. We cannot, then, automatically assume that any activity on its own will meet this requirement.

Definition II.a. is more restrictive and does not claim that any activity can be sacred but it does say that if an activity can be understood as directed by a divine source, it is then religious. Unfortunately, there have been some who have claimed that a divine authority told them to commit acts of great violence. Surely, we cannot consider such acts to be sacred. II.d. is in a similar category. By stating that religion is what *should* be our ultimate concern assumes that someone will instinctively know what should be their ultimate concern. If my ultimate concern is whether or not I will have a date this weekend can you assume that I will know that this really should not be the true ultimate concern? It also assumes that one has the luxury to focus on spirituality as an ultimate concern. The ultimate concern of someone who is starving may be radically different from the person who has a steady income. Definition II.e. makes a similar assumption as the previous two by assuming that someone's genuine perspective will be focused beyond the ego. We cannot assume to know what is or should be a person's perspective but we should be able to come up with a clearer idea of what a religious perspective should be. Whitehead's definition (II.h.) runs into a similar problem in assuming that one's solitariness will always be oriented towards the spiritual. The score card now reads:

I.a.	I.b.	I.c.	I.d.	I.e.	I.f.	I.g.			
II.a.	II.b.	II.c.	II.d.	II.e.	IIf.	IIg.	II.h.	II.i.	II.j.
III.a.	III.b.	III.c.	III.d.						
IV.a.	IV.b.	IV.c.							

Our third limiting factor is to find a definition that helps us to look at a particular practice or philosophy and determine if it can be considered a religion. To do that, a definition must distinguish between what is a religion and what is religiousness. Although interesting and thought provoking, some of the above definitions describe the feeling of being religious rather than give us clues as to how we can truly identify a religion. One of the best examples is number III.c. by Einstein. He describes what the feeling of religiousness is to him but his definition could not be used to determine if a particular practice or set of practices can be defined as a religion. Both II.b. and II.c. do essentially the same thing by describing what religiousness is but not what a *particular* religion is or does. Number II.f. also falls into this same category by describing a particular belief rather than setting a test for any number of theologies. Definition III.a. describes Camus' feelings about the sacred but, again, does not offer us a litmus test for other practices while III.d. is a description of Emerson's understanding of a what a religious person should experience. The score card now reads:

I.a.	I.b.	I.c.	I.d.	I.e.	I.f.	I.g.			
II.a.	II.b.	II.c.	II.d.	II.e.	II.f.	II.g.	II.h.	II.i.	II.j.
III.a.	III.b.	III.c.	III.d.						
IV.a.	IV.b.	IV.c.							

We are now left with six definitions that have made it through the three filters. In order to find a good definition, however, I want to apply yet another series of tests. I am going to compare the remaining definitions to four test cases: Christianity, Buddhism, The Freemasons (Masons), and the Boy Scouts. Most people, I believe, would agree that both Christianity and Buddhism are religions while the Masons and the Boy Scouts are not. If any of the definitions left to examine can successfully include the first two organizations while, at the same time, exclude the second two then we will accept the definition as workable. Before we can begin this test, however, we should be clear about the groups we are using as test cases by stating clear definitions for each.

Christianity is based on the life and teachings of Jesus described in the four books called the Gospels which are part of the Bible. Christians believe that Jesus was resurrected after his death and that he is one of the three persons of the one God (the others being God and the Holy Spirit). Christianity is a monotheistic religion that believes that all people have sinned and are, therefore, separated from

God. Salvation is found by accepting and following the teachings of Jesus (called the Christ). Practices include prayer, Bible study, baptism, and attendance to church on Sundays. There is a hierarchical priesthood who leads services and provides teachings.

Buddhism is based on the teachings of Guatama Siddhartha (called the Buddha) who taught that the purpose of life is to avoid suffering by releasing desires and to end the cycle of rebirth by gaining enlightenment. Buddhism does not have a central god although later developments recognized celestial buddhas and boddhisatvas. Its central text is called the Pali Canon - a collection of early Buddhist writings. The main practice is to seek enlightenment through meditation. Ritual is used both personally and communally. There is a hierarchical structure of priests who lead services and provide teaching.

The Freemasons are a fraternal organization. Membership is restricted to men only and each one must confess a belief in a Supreme Being (though not strictly defined) and in the resurrection of the body. Members are expected to attend regular meetings in organized lodges and to provide community service through their lodge. There are a minimum of three degrees of learning in Masonry with additional degrees possible. The Masons hold up the concepts of brotherly love, relief, and truth as their primary principles. Ritual is involved in meetings and in the initiation of degrees. Leaders are structured in hierarchical levels of experience and training based on degrees.

The Boy Scouts is an organization for young men ages 11 - 17. Though not stated specifically on their web site, members are expected to confess a belief in a single God. The Boy Scout motto starts with the words: "On my honor I will do my best to do my duty to God and my country..." Members are expected to attend regular meetings in which they receive training toward the attainment of merit badges. Merit badges are used by the members to move up in the system of six basic degrees. Ritual is kept to a minimum, however. Leaders both within the packs (organizing groups) and the adult leaders are structured hierarchically. Practices include outdoor training such as camping, hiking, and orientation skills.

Now, we will test the remaining definitions with these test cases. Because definition I.c. allows a choice between a cause, principle, or a set of beliefs, any of our four test groups would fit the definition. Therefore, I.c. does not give us a good way to distinguish between them. Certainly, Christians and Buddhists are committed to their beliefs. The Masons may hold to their principles of brotherly love, relief, and truth with great ardor and faith but such conviction does not a religion make. Similarly, the Boy Scouts may believe that their cause of shaping young men is a great one but it does not define them as a religious movement.

At first glance, definition I.d. would seem to fall into the same trap as I.c. except that it contains the word *worship*. Wikipedia defines worship as "specific acts of religious devotion, typically directed to one or more deities." Since they use the word *typically* we can assume that a deity is not necessary for worship to take place but it does seem to imply that what receives devotion is something beyond and greater than the ego self in a way that a deity might represent. Trying to define *religious devotion* here would lead us into some circuitous meanderings. Let us assume, instead, that religious devotion means devotion to something sacred. With this in mind, we can see that this definition does apply to Christianity and Buddhism since they both involve worship of something sacred. Though the Masons and the Boy Scouts require belief in a Supreme Being, neither includes adoration of that being in their practices and meetings. Definition I.g. also separates Christianity and Buddhism by requiring supernatural claims about the human condition that are then pursued through devotional practices. Definition III.b. is similar in nature to these two and, so, would also work.

Definition IV.a. focuses on right purpose and good works which, certainly, are part of the practices of both Christianity and Buddhism but so are they central to the works of the Masons and the Boy Scouts. Both these groups center their principles on morality and both groups do charitable works in the community making this definition unsuitable for us. Definition IV.c. is markedly different than most of the other definitions listed above. Instead of defining religion in a bold sweeping statement, it contains a list of requirements. IV.c. is a definition based on function more than on description. There are several of its requirements that do apply to all four of our test cases but there are some that do not. For example, though members of the Masons and Boy Scouts may pray, prayer is not part of the standard practices of either group and both the Masons and the Boy Scouts do not require their members to prescribe to a particular world view or to organize their lives according to such a view. Definition II.j. centers on the use of sacred symbols to establish a world view which we have already mentioned is not a feature of our two non-religious test cases. The scorecard is now reduced to the following:

I.a.	I.b.	I.c.	I.d.	I.e.	I.f.	I.g.			
II.a.	II.b.	II.c.	II.d.	II.e.	IIf.	IIg.	II.h.	II.i.	II.j.
III.a.	III.b.	III.c.	III.d.						
IV.a.	IV.b.	IV.c.							

Comparing Terms

We can now compare our remaining five definitions with our definition of Paganism to determine if Paganism can indeed be considered a religion. We will begin with the definition offered by Webster's Dictionary (I.d.). This definition has two stipulations for something to qualify as a religion: 1) a code of ethics, and 2) a philosophy. Paganism has ethical principles though there is no single codified creed to which all Pagans must adhere. The second Pillar states that all choices in spirituality and in living are to be made freely but with all possible consequences in mind. In addition, many Pagans (especially Wiccans) follow the principle of "no harm" which is similar to the concept of Ahimsa - a central ethical principle for the religions of Buddhism, Jainism, and Hinduism. Paganism has a system of belief stated in the first and third Pillars - divinity exists in all things and is ever moving and ever changing. Worship of the divine is accomplished through personal and group ritual.

The Wikipedia definition I.g. has three stipulations: 1) the religion should have beliefs and practices that are centered upon an understanding of reality that has a supernatural basis, 2) the religion should have a morality based on that reality, and 3) the religion should have a set of practices such as prayer, ritual and "religious law" which is also based on that understanding of reality. The word *supernatural* often implies images of ghosts, strange powers, and luminous beings but the word simply means that which is above and beyond nature. We run into a problem here with the word natural. Most Pagans believe that all things are part of nature but this is really a new way of thinking about the term nature. Even Spirit, energy, or the gods are all part of this modern concept of nature but I do not think that is how the nature is meant when most people use the word supernatural. When people say "nature", they often mean the empirical or those things which can be personally experienced through the senses. To those who hold to the traditional meaning of the word nature, a tree is something natural because it can be touched and seen but a tree's energy field would not be natural. Most people cannot see the energy fields of living beings and so they are not experienced and classified as part of nature. In this manner, the energy field of a living being would be termed supernatural. If we take the word to have this meaning, then Paganism fits into this first part of the Wikipedia definition. The first Pillar of Paganism says that the divine (Energy, Spirit, God, Goddess, Higher Self, etc) is both within and beyond all things making it both natural and supernatural. As we have discussed in the previous paragraph, many Pagans practice a moral code based on an understanding that all things are sacred and should be treated in such a manner. Few would call it a religious "law" and would probably bristle at the harsh sound of the phrase itself but, nonetheless, most Pagans feel it is important to put their theology into practice through their daily interactions with others. Pagans also have a set of practices based on this understanding of universal reverence. Some Pagans pray in the same manner as people in other religions do while other Pagans do not - but most have some form of personal or group ritual practice that they engage in on a regular basis.

Clifford Geertz was an anthropologist whose work in remote cultures led to his unique but lengthy definition of religion. His definition has become rather well known and respected to those who study religion, though, so I wanted to include it in our list of possible definitions. The focus of his definition is on the use of sacred symbols. Disregarding the sexist language and the overall skepticism embedded in his definition (he was born in 1926 after all), we can see the importance he places on the use of symbols to create a world view and a purpose for living within that view. Since this is the case let us take a moment to look at the significance of sacred symbols which can have several important functions in a spiritual outlook.

The Purpose of Religious Symbols

1) to reveal an understanding of reality or the sacred which is not otherwise experienced empirically
2) to contain a multiplicity of meanings
3) to express the inexpressible
4) to help provide meaning to existence.

In books about religion you will often see a paragraph dealing with the difficulties of trying to describe religious experiences using words. That is because words are symbols which can have a variety of meanings. For example, if I say the word *bow* to you, how do you know if I am talking about the front of a ship, a way of introducing myself to you, something I put on top of a package, or something used to fire off an arrow? I can put the word in a sentence and provide a context but the meaning may still be obscure. If I say "I have come to offer you a bow because you are such a good friend," am I presenting you with a weapon or a frilly fabric knot? Even if I say "I got a package today with such a lovely bow on it," you and I might know that the bow was some knotted object on my package but, unless I described it to you in detail, we would probably have different ideas of what that bow looked like. If a word as simple as *bow* can have so many meanings consider the multitude of meanings associated with a religious word such as "god."

Graphic symbols can be even more obscure than words. Consider the swastika. That particular symbol has come to mean hatred, anti-Semitism, and intolerance because it was used by the Nazis but it is also a symbol sacred to Jainism - a religion that combines elements of both Hinduism and Buddhism. To the Jains, the swastika represents the motion of the universe and the intersection of the heavenly and the earthly. One symbol can have many completely different meanings to different people and can express much more than a few words could ever hope to do. Sacred symbols are deeply connected to inner feelings and, through these emotions, can help provide meaning to life. Both meanings of the swastika are related to deep seated feelings and ideas: one of great hatred and another of a mystical connection to all beings. These are complex concepts related to deep emotions but they can be attached to a single symbol.

Symbols, then, can play a great role in helping a group of people define a religious concept and remind them of those concepts when they see it. The cross represents to Christians the great sacrifice made by Jesus to save humanity from sin. Whenever a Christian sees a cross, the religious teachings of his or her faith will be remembered. The symbol can serve as a reminder on how one should act and live according to the religious teaching associated with it. Paganism has many symbols that can have the same function as those of other religions. Though not all Pagans recognize the pentagram as a sacred symbol, many do. The pentagram can represent the sacredness of all people by representing the body and its five senses, five appendages, and five fingers and toes reminding us that people are equally part of the divine. It can symbolize the fourfold nature of Earth (often further symbolized by the four classical elements) with Spirit as the fifth "quintessential" element of the universe showing that the supernatural and the celestial as well as the natural and the earthly are all part of the same circle of life. It can represent the planet Venus with its associations of the feminine and love and it can represent a star of hope. The pentagram can serve as a reminder to Pagans that all things are connected through Spirit, that we are all children of Earth, and that we should act with this universal connectedness in mind.

The definition by York (III.b.) is somewhat similar to the last two in that it also mentions the word *supernatural* and discusses the use of suggestions and techniques in the same way that Geertz mentions symbols. We have already talked about the use of the word supernatural and how it can be applied to Paganism. Suggestions and techniques are, of course, principles and practices which can be represented through symbolism and passed on through teaching.

Cline's definition (IV.c), as I have mentioned earlier, is a bit different than the rest. It is a list of requirements that Cline feels will define a religion. In order to determine if Paganism fulfills his definition we will have to look at each of the nine requirements separately.

1) A belief in something sacred. This is an easy one. Most Pagans believe that everything is sacred.

2) A distinction between sacred and profane objects. This one is not so easy. If we believe that everything is sacred, then how can we make a distinction between sacred and profane? Pagans actually do make such a distinction. When making the sacred circle in rituals, the circle is meant to separate sacred space from other space and often special tools are used to symbolize sacred truths. But, you might ask, if everywhere and everything is sacred, how can you claim one space or thing to be sacred while another is not. All things and all space is sacred and that is why a sacred circle can be made anywhere and any object (including stones and sticks, for example) can be considered sacred instruments. Pagans do not have to meet in a church to find sacred space nor do they need specially made objects (although some like them). Any space and any object that you choose can be recognized as sacred. Here is the difference though: through ritual and intention nothing is really *made* sacred, it becomes only *recognized* as sacred. The distinction is one of awareness and attention. Most of us have a limited capacity for recognizing all things as sacred all the time so we focus our awareness on certain times, certain places, and certain objects as being sacred so that we can commune with that sacredness for a limited time. At other times we must return to our routines and our sense of ordinary everyday existence in order to seek balance and to do the things we need to do in order to survive. This reality is part of the many cycles of life.

3) Ritual acts focused on sacred objects. If nothing else, almost all Pagans are focused on doing some type of personal or group form of ritual. Some use fancy tools while others use common objects to provide symbolism in their rituals.

4) A moral code believed to have a sacred or supernatural basis. We have discussed previously the moral code of "no harm" used by many Pagans. Even those without an explicit code will feel obligated to treat others with a sense of moral justice because it is difficult to harm others when you know that every person, every creature, and every thing is part of the same sacred substance. Because this substance (Spirit, energy, consciousness, etc.) is beyond the empirical, we may call it supernatural.

5) Characteristically religious feelings, which tend to be aroused in the presence of sacred objects and during the practice of ritual. Cline assumes that we all know what characteristic religious feelings feel like. Texts on mysticism of many different religions often characterize a sense of being connected to something greater as a religious feeling so I will assume that this is what is meant here as well. The purpose of most Pagan rituals is to help the practitioner celebrate the cycles of life and the universe and to help him or her experience a personal connection to the ultimate reality. Pagan rituals often involve methods of achieving a state of altered consciousness and use elements of sacred theater and play to help transport practitioners to a level of awareness which is beyond the everyday experience. Sometimes sacred tools, clothing, language, and symbols are used to help add to the overall experience.

6) Prayer and other forms of communication with the supernatural. The internet site Wordnet defines prayer as both the act of communicating with a deity and an earnest or urgent request. Often people understand the term to mean both things: prayer is a request made to a deity. There are four forms of traditional prayer: prayer to ask for something, prayer to pay homage, prayer to ask for forgiveness, or prayer to express thanks. Some Pagans are deists and some are not. That is to say, some Pagans believe in the existence of gods (usually at least a male and female entity) and some do not. To complicate matters further, some Pagans speak of the gods but understand the terms to be metaphors instead of representations of living beings. Those that believe in gods may pray in the traditional manner of making a request to those deities. That request may come in the form of a set of words meant to be heard by the intended deity or it may be spoken as part of the central section of a ritual meant to make a connection with that deity. However, some forms of prayer done by Pagans can be less traditional. Some Pagans make requests in the form of what is known as "directing one's intention" in what is often referred to as "magick" (spelled with a with a "k" to distinguish it from simple illusion). Some Pagans believe that, since we are all part of the same energy force, we can apply our will to that energy in order to influence events. Because Pagans understand that science is an equal part of the reality of the universe, they also understand that magick cannot go against the laws of physics (the laws of Nature). Therefore, the truth of the matter is that no one person can simply do or have whatever is desired whenever it is desired but it may be possible to make some sort of influence on the fabric of energies that make up our existence. This is a complex subject that many books have devoted many pages to but, suffice it to say that magick is a more active and personal way to make a request to the universe - it is a unique form of prayer. Pagans may enact a personal or group ritual to make a request to the universe, to offer praise and gratitude to Earth or the universe for providing the necessities of life, to make amends for mistakes made, or to celebrate the many cycles and changes of life.

7) A world view, or a general picture of the world as a whole and the place of the individual therein. This picture contains some specification of an over-all purpose or point of the world and an indication of how the individual fits into it. Paganism offers a world view that is both positive and inclusive and can be seen as an alternative to some of the traditional world views. Pagans see everything as sacred. There is no need for a "chosen people" or one sacred book that tells the truth above all others. Paganism accepts the reality of the universe; there is no separation between religion and science since both express part of reality. Paganism does not deny the body or the senses nor does it claim that we are born with a need to redeem ourselves. The point of life to a Pagan is to live - to live fully! As we dance, so does Spirit dance and exist. Spirit is manifest through all life so that it may also be alive. We are here, all of us, to experience life in all its many forms. It is our responsibility to choose to live well and to take care of ourselves and to care for Earth and all of life as best we can. Spirit will continue on in some form or another. We are dependent upon the energy of life but it is not dependent on us. Therefore, we need to be always conscious of our choices and the consequences they have on our lives, the lives of others, and the environment.

8) A more or less total organization of one's life based on the world view. If you read the previous paragraph then you will have already seen how Paganism fulfills this requirement. The Pagan world view requires that Pagans see their lives in a different way than has been traditionally learned. A Pagan organizes his or her life around the choices that he or she makes. Those choices will be based on the ideas of universal sacredness and personal responsibility. Pagans also organize their lives around the cycles of Earth and the universe. The phases of the moon, the change of the seasons, the milestones of life, the location of the stars, and other cycles take on a spiritual significance and meaning in the life of the Pagan. Living within those cycles is part of the joy of living. It is a unique and exciting way to see the world. The universe is no longer an empty machine ticking away like some colossal clock, it is alive and full of energy that is shared by all beings. Instead of seeing the ordinariness of every day, the Pagan sees the constant changes and surprises that await every open heart and mind. Every day is always different because everything is always in motion and is in the process of changing.

9) A social group bound together by the above. Some Pagans practice alone and some practice within groups. Most do both to some degree. Because some Pagans gather together and some do not does not disqualify Paganism for this requirement of the definition. After all, there are people who say they are Christian but do not regularly attend church. The religion provides the opportunities for social and spiritual growth though its members may or may not take advantage of them. Pagans have open gatherings such as study groups and public rituals and there are more closed groups such as covens and private rituals and practices. There are also more informal Pagan gatherings in almost every major metropolitan area in the democratic world and, of course, there is always the internet. The opportunities for Pagan growth and connection are there.

Paganism As a Spirituality

Many times I have heard people (especially younger people) say "I am spiritual but not religious." What does this mean? When pressed further, the same people often say that they are not interested in being a part of an "organized religion." Since most of the people I know were raised or were influenced by a Christian upbringing, what they usually mean is that they no longer wish to go to church services but want to maintain a personal religious practice or understanding of their own. Not all religions are organized in the same way, however. Though Christianity (especially Catholicism) has a clear hierarchy, not all religions are so structured. None of the definitions of religion we observed above discuss formal structure as a requirement of religion. Those definitions that made it through our filters did have a common assumption expressed in the words practice, worship, techniques, and ritual acts: religion has at least some kind of expression shared by people with similar beliefs. Wikipedia explains that "spirituality, in a narrow sense, concerns itself with matters of the spirit." Such matters must be an internal experience. We may say, then, that spirituality is an inner experience and a personal relationship with the divine while religion is the external expression of that relationship. Paganism has both qualities. The Three Pillars express a particular world view that can be internalized and become a mode for living in harmony with the cycles of Earth and the universe and for acting with others. This makes Paganism a spirituality. This Pagan understanding of the world can be expressed through prayer, ritual, magick, or simple practices that honor Earth, all beings, and the cycles of life. These activities can be shared with small or large groups of like-minded people which makes Paganism also a religion.

Conclusion

As you can see, I have gone a long way to make a short point - I believe Paganism is a religion and no less a religion than those often considered major world religions. It is also a spirituality and can be practiced as one or both. The one undeniable difference between Paganism and other religions is that the major world religions have more people who claim to be adherents than does Paganism but I believe that this will change because not only is Paganism a religion and a spirituality, it is a deep spiritual philosophy and practice that is well suited for the postmodern world of the 21st Century.

Chapter Two

Paganism and Postmodernism

"The central hallmark of postmodern cultural expression is pluralism." ~ *Grenz*

The Three Eras of Modern History

The second point I want to make with this text is that Paganism is a religion that is needed in this age of Postmodernism. In order to make the point, however, we will need to understand a little about the trends of our current culture which have been characterized in the term "postmodernism." Philosophers have come to recognize three ages of modern times. They are termed *Pre-Modern*, *Modern*, and *Postmodern*. The Modern era has also been called the Industrial Age because it began around the same time that the Western culture developed machines for industry. As machines were invented, so was a feeling that the universe was nothing more than a giant machine itself that was set in motion by God and left alone to its own devices. Philosophically, the Modern era began earlier with the theories of Descartes and Newton who helped bring about what became known as The Enlightenment. The theorists of the Enlightenment championed reason over everything else; it became the primary way to know the universe. People believed that everything could eventually be known through reason and scientific experimentation since it was also the age of the scientific method. Truth was anything that could be tested. It was a time when the powers of rulers and churches were questioned and many reforms in both government and religion were undertaken. Man, not God, became the ultimate force of the planet. Nature was seen as an unlimited resource for mankind. The age before the Modern era is called, of course, Pre-Modern and was influenced primarily by the ruling authorities of the Church, the aristocracy, and the various rulers of countries.

The Modern era brought about many needed reforms and changes to the sometimes oppressive rule of Church authorities and the monarchy. Although the great historical document and precursor of the U.S. Constitution, the Magna Carta, predated the Enlightenment, the idea of human rights for all people flourished with the theories and subsequent revolutions of the Enlightenment period. Modernism encouraged multiple perspectives on many subjects and ideas like a democratic government and a separation of church and state became an eventual realities for most of the countries of Europe and the United States. The sciences flourished as well during this time. Having escaped many of the earlier controls of religion, scientists were able to explore and develop new and controversial theories which helped to expand our understanding of the world. There were downsides to Modernity, however. The idea that mankind is in control of nature has led to environmental degradation that threatens life on our home planet. The dominance of reason has developed into a suspicion of anything other than that which can be understood by the mind. The idea that the heart, the body, and the soul are secondary to the mind can lead to a way of living that is devoid of a wholeness of experience and existence. Mystery is feared and avoided because it cannot be reasoned away. The rights of the individual have been emphasized so much that individualism is championed over cooperation. Competition and force are seen as the primary means to achieving one's needs.

Starting in the middle of the Nineteenth Century, a shift began to take place in Western society. The change was further influenced and propelled by the advent of personal computers. The emphasis of the culture went from a dependence on machines to an emphasis on information. This shift began to turn a conglomerate of nations into one truly global village. Major cultural shifts really took off in the 1970's, however, and brought about even more new ways of seeing the world. Instead of being the primary method of interfacing with the world, reason took a seat alongside emotions and feelings. Experience became equally important to rationalization. Domination and hierarchy became despised while cooperation and understanding became the new rallying cries of the era. Nature went from being an endless resource to a fragile ecosystem. The effects of our years of misuse and exploitation of the land, sea, and air revealed themselves as horrid scars upon the blue green marble called home and awakened a new sensibility within us. Truth and reality became subjective and differing opinions were welcomed and respected. There was no longer a belief in the single truth that was waiting to be discovered through rational analysis and scientific testing. This shift in the way we viewed our selves and our world would be called the beginning of the Postmodern era.

Postmodernism and Religion

The traditional religions of the West have always been resistant to change. When the Enlightenment began, new scientific discoveries were viewed as challenges to church doctrine. Scientists were discredited and their theories were ridiculed. With the advent of Modernism, church populations began to splinter and decline. Churches began to lose the power and control they once held over the lives of others. There was a rise in humanism and skepticism but religion did not completely disappear. Many of the Enlightenment thinkers did not become atheists. Instead, they called themselves Deists; they still believed in a god but their god was not an active agent in the world. For them, God set the great clock of the universe in motion and then retired away to a far corner of the heavens to watch his creation evolve. Man became responsible for himself and had to take an active role in making society better for all people.

Though the structure of the church had to change to accommodate a more secular society, there was much about modernism that still coincided with traditional religious thought. The church had, for a long time, treated women as secondary to men. The male dominated society of the Enlightenment was no different in its attitude toward women. Though societies became more democratic, the right to vote for women would come long after the establishment of those governments. The same was true for minorities. Equality was usually reserved for the white majority. Minority groups are, even today, still struggling to gain truly equal treatment and access to society. God was still seen as a domineering male figure who was separate from man and who controlled events from beyond. Though many of the Modernists appreciated nature and its immense beauty, it was still seen as a resource for the betterment of mankind. The mind and body remained separate with the mind being the higher faculty. The body was only a dirty vessel capable of great sin and a distraction from the greater pursuit of reason. Anything that raised feelings and emotions was considered crude and indecent. Things like sexuality were considered to be an animal-like behavior which, of course, man was above.

Postmodernism brought about changes in perspective that were even further away from the viewpoints of the traditional religions. One of the greatest changes was to see the sacred in all things - a viewpoint known as immanence. Postmodern thinkers began to see the sacred as an essential quality that existed in all things and all people equally. This equality was extended to all beings including women, minorities and even all animals. The feminine quality was no longer seen as a source of weakness and sin but became something to be honored. Women's spirituality helped change the face of God into the Goddess and the traditional domains of the feminine - sexuality, love of the body, finding joy through the senses, appreciating beauty, seeking cooperation, and acting with compassion - were also embraced. This sense of equality also honored the individual opinion and worked toward decision making through consensus and team building. Hierarchies were viewed as coercive and oppressive.

Many people of the Postmodern era were influenced by Einstein's famous principle concerning mass and energy: $E=MC^2$. In this equation, E stands for energy, M stands for mass, and C represents the thing that Einstein thought was the one constant of the universe - the speed of light (186, 000 miles per second). In essence, the equation states that all things are comprised of energy at various states of vibration. What we call mass is simply energy that is vibrating at a slow rate. By this theory, any mass that can be accelerated to a speed which equals the square of the speed of light would become pure energy. Such concepts required a faith in the mysterious. We cannot see the vibrations of energy in solid objects and we do not experience the world in this way but we can still accept it as reality. The world of quantum physics created a whole new way of seeing the universe as something that is strange and alive with qualities that are very different from day to day experiences.

Though the traditional religions shared some philosophical ideas with Modernism, Postmodernism turned out to be a different matter. Instead of searching for common ground, the new trends were looked upon by many church leaders as signs that the society was moving further from the direction set by God even as pews continued to empty. There was one major exception to this pattern: the evangelical Christian churches and fundamentalism in many religions began to thrive and grow. Unlike some other traditions, the evangelicals knew how to tap into the new paradigm. They used contemporary music and encouraged their members to move their bodies. Religion became a personal experience as each person was encouraged to seek and be filled with the spirit of God. The new mega-churches sought to take care of the whole person and family. They offered child care, counseling, dating services, health programs, meals, and personalized study groups. People of all colors and backgrounds were embraced into the flock. People at all levels were encouraged to speak and to take part in the leadership of the church. Only the essential theology remained the same.

There needed to be a truly alternative religious choice to appeal to those of the Postmodern era who, for whatever reason, could not align themselves with the traditional religions. That new religion would have to possess certain qualities that would reflect the new times. A Postmodern religion would need to be personal, inclusive, holistic, and pluralistic. The religion would have to be personal by having a core set of values that could be explored and understood individually. There could be no central creed to which all members would have to swear their allegiance but there would be some general agreed upon points. Questioning and seeking personal truth would be encouraged. Individual members of the religion would be able to practice on their own if they chose but could also participate in group activities. The religious experience could be sought either way. The religion would have to emphasize how to find a joyous way of living that included practices to help people personally experience that joy.

The new religion would have to be inclusive. It would need to embrace all the different ways of experiencing reality. There would be no need to separate religion, art, metaphysics, and science because each would be seen as part of the total fabric of truth. The new religion would be open to all people; there would be no need to claim to be part of the chosen people. Men and women of all races and economic backgrounds would be embraced equally and welcome to participate as would the gay, bisexual, and transgendered. Human rights would be not only honored but would be considered a religious imperative. That sense of equality would also extend beyond humans to animals and to all the living beings of Earth as well as Earth herself.

The new religion would need to be holistic. The whole self would need to be engaged in the religious practice and methods of worship. It would not be enough to just appeal to the mind; people must feel free to move and sing, laugh, and play, feel and experience the sacred both on a personal level and a group level. The individual spiritual experience would be emphasized over the adherence to dogma and formulas for practice. Like any religion, however, this personal experience would have to be put in a universal context to avoid becoming simply a means to gratify the ego. To accomplish this, the religion would have to be able to embrace both the concepts of immanence and transcendence.

For far too long, immanence and transcendence have been seen as distant polar opposites in theological discussions. In line with the Modernist way of thinking, a dualistic approach to each of these two ways of experiencing the divine has led to decades of heated debate. The Postmodern way of thinking, however, does not see all things in straight lines and complete opposites; not everything is simply this or that. It is my belief that a Postmodern religion needs to be able to embrace both concepts. Immanence is the belief that the divine exists in all things. Transcendence is the belief that the divine is greater and beyond all living things. Traditional religions have emphasized the need for mankind to transcend existence and connect to a divine being that is separate from his own creation. Newer religions and theologies have emphasized the need to recognize all life as a part of the divine. For them, there is no separation between the sacred and the things that exist because of it. Immanence is a deep and joyous experience of the unity of all beings and of being part of the creative experience of the universe. Exclusively following either theological perspective leads to problems, however. For those who pursue the transcendent divine to the extreme, the need to escape from a cultural context can lead to a neglect of the needs of life and of others. There becomes a need to divide those who are "saved" from those who are not. A separate all-powerful god can become an excuse to ignore personal and social responsibilities (God will take care of everything). The transcendent can become obsessed in pleasing God rather than in becoming authentic. Pure immanence can result in some spiritual difficulties as well. Immanence to the extreme can lead to religious selfishness and arrogance. One might think that if I am the divine then I can do whatever I want. Moreover, if one believes that he contains the same awesome creative power of the universe then he believes that he can have whatever he wants whenever he wants it. The immanent can become obsessed in satisfying his own needs and then wrapping those selfish pursuits in spiritual language in order to justify his personal egotistical pursuits to himself and others.

There are, of course, positive attributes to both immanence and transcendence. Transcendence can help us to go beyond ourselves and our basic needs and can help us seek the greater good whereas immanence can help us to see ourselves and all things as possessing an inherent self worth and value. It is possible to view those two positions not as extreme opposites but as two ways of seeing the same thing. One can see the divine as both the essence of all things and yet that which is also a greater unity. Consider the fish in the ocean. Like all living beings on this planet, the fish contains within it a great amount of water and, yet, also swims within a great ocean of water. Water is both within and beyond it. We can both possess the great energy of the universe within us and also recognize that energy as being greater and more mysterious than our individual selves. The Postmodern religion is able to grasp and teach one how to live within such a seemingly paradoxical theology.

Postmodernism and Paganism

As Postmodernism began to take hold as a major shift in the culture, several new religions developed that would come to embrace the new ideals. One of the fastest growing new religions became known as Neo-Paganism. Modern Paganism has all three qualities needed for a Postmodern religion; it is personal, inclusive, and holistic. Paganism does not contain a single creed. As I have outlined in the Three Pillars, there are some common assumptions made about the universe and the condition of humans in the universe but individual Pagans are free to define the particulars of those assumptions for themselves. Some Pagans are deistic (usually polytheistic) while some are nature mystics and others are atheistic and might be considered more humanistic in their ideology. Some Pagans prefer to practice strictly on their own while others prefer to gather in ritualistic and social groups and many others combine individual with group worship. There are no set formulas for practice and Pagans are free to design altars and their own spiritual methodologies in any way they choose. Paganism is a positive religion and practitioners often seek a personal connection to the creative and joyful energy of the universe that helps to foster a sense of inner worth while also developing a need to be a force of positive change and growth in the world.

Paganism is inclusive. Since all things are equally part of the divine, there is no distinction between those who can be considered holy from those who cannot be saved. All people, all living things, and all of Earth is considered equally sacred. Pagans realize that there will always be people with different religious viewpoints (notice that the title of this book is "Paganism: *A* religion for the 21st Century" not "Paganism *the* religion for the 21st Century"). Other religions are not seen as competition but are viewed as different ways of experiencing the ultimate truth. Any religion which does not advocate causing harm is tolerated and appreciated. In fact, all ways of knowing the universe are to be equally appreciated. The sciences, the arts, metaphysics, and religions are seen as different ways to understand the mysteries of the universe and of the complexity of who we are. The strange and quirky world that has been revealed through quantum physics can be accepted and appreciated as much as the mysteries of the occult may be. Each person is free to choose how much to learn and embrace for themselves.

Paganism is holistic. It stresses practices that involve the whole body. Rituals often involve moving, dancing, and singing, and can include trance work and altered states of consciousness. There are plenty of deep mysteries to ponder mentally and questioning and exploration are always encouraged but the mind is not the only part of the self that can experience the divine. The body can be encouraged to move, the heart can be encouraged to explore complex feelings, and the soul can be encouraged to find deep universal and cosmic connections. Each practitioner is free to do as little or as much as he or she likes or feels comfortable (although going beyond the comfort zone can also be encouraged by Pagan teachers and study groups). In fact, Pagans often see all the different ways of understanding reality as part of the whole fabric of truth. Like a quilt, each area can be examined separately but gains greater meaning when the entire result can be seen as a whole. The sciences help us to understand the physical world but do not reveal the entire picture and the same can be said for religion which helps us to understand the metaphysical world but needs to be related to the knowledge gained in the sciences as well. Psychology helps us to understand the mind while the arts help us to understand the many facets of our complex feelings. Paganism does not dismiss any of these ways of knowing and understanding the world.

Though some Pagans tend to embrace immanence while others are more transcendent, Paganism has the ability to be both immanent and transcendent. I have already expressed my opinion that Pagans should be willing to embrace both means of relating to the universe. Immanence allows us to experience the deep inner joy of being equally part of the divine while transcendence gives us a spiritual direction in which to reach our higher selves and the greater unity of all things. Traditional religions have always been uncomfortable with immanence and many of those who have left those religions have abandoned transcendence as well but such a decision can lead to the proverbial baby and bath water dilemma. One can experience transcendence without the need of a separate male god figure. Postmodernism has become uncomfortable with transcendence because it has traditionally been linked to controlling hierarchies that have been in charge of telling people how to transcend the sin-filled body and world. One can experience immanence and still develop a voluntarily accepted connection and responsibility to others.

Why the World Needs Religion and Paganism

Paganism may be a Postmodern religion - but is it necessary? Is religion even needed at all in this new world view? I think so. Religion is especially needed in times of great change. Another reason that evangelical churches have been growing lately is because people often seek something as an anchor during times of rapid change. By connecting with the universe in the same way that a boat might get tied to a dock during stormy seas, religion can help us find meaning in the change and give us something to hang on to as we go through the storm and look for the clearing on the other side.

Religion and spirituality helps us to go beyond mere satisfaction of the ego and find connections with each other and with the essence of the universe. Religion, along with the arts and the sciences, is also a way of understanding the whole self. More than that, religion can help us understand some of the mysteries of the universe. Science has not yet uncovered answers to mysteries such as: why we are here, why we suffer, and why we die. Religion can help us define who we are to ourselves and others and how we should interact with one another. Religion, through ritual and spiritual practices, can take us beyond our day to day existence.

Paganism can help us to do all those things but it is especially needed in these modern times for additional reasons. Because of our past attitude toward Nature we have created an ecological disaster that threatens all life on this planet. Paganism can help us to regain an attitude of reverence toward Earth and all her creatures. Restoring health to the planet will require a deep desire to heal her and to change the way we live. A spiritual connection with Earth helps to establish a deep bond between Earth and people and, through Paganism, that bond can be extended to all living beings. Paganism also teaches tolerance toward all other people regardless of their background or religion. This type of religious tolerance is sorely needed in this world where many of the wars and global conflicts are centered on religious differences. It may be too much to ask that all religious people be tolerant but if at least one religion can model tolerance there may be hope for more global cooperation. Another reason Paganism is needed in the Postmodern world is that its lack of central hierarchy and its openness to individual interpretations of its basic principles allows it to be more flexible and pliable. It can adapt more readily to changes in society and to individual temperaments. Deists, atheists, agnostics, humanists, nature mystics, and others can all equally be Pagan practitioners and can adapt their practices as each one grows individually and through their own cultures. Traditional religions constantly feel as if they are in conflict with modern society because they refuse to change with them. They are quick to blame changes on evil influences rather than the expanding and growing consciousness of humanity. Paganism has no need to control people and keep them locked into a possibly stagnant world view.

Change is a constant in the universe. As people continue to exist on Earth they will continue to develop, grow, and expand into new levels of consciousness. The rise of Postmodernism is part of that development. People and their institutions need to come to terms with these changes or risk being ineffectual and out of step with reality. Paganism is a religion that is both a product of Postmodernism and is a way of helping people deal with the changes that this era brings upon us.

Chapter Three

What It Means (and does not mean) To Be Pagan

When men stop believing in God, it isn't that they then believe in nothing: they believe in everything. ~ Umberto Eco

Becoming Pagan

Pagans have no procedure for becoming Pagan. If you agree with the Three Pillars and wish to be identified as a Pagan (whether publicly or privately) then you are a Pagan. If you want to be a practicing Pagan then you will need to either learn, adapt, or create your own practices that reflect your personal Pagan theology. Pagans respect individual spiritual pursuits and the religions of others so there is no need to try and convert people or to have some type of conversion event. That does not meant that you could not create one of your own if you felt you needed it. Some Pagans do a special ritual in which they dedicate themselves to to their spiritual path but none is ever necessary.

There is no conversion or coercion. Though there are now children who are being raised Pagan (or are at least being raised by Pagan parents), most Pagans have come from another religious tradition or culture. Even those who may be raised Pagan may find that the current culture can seem to be at odds with the Pagan way of seeing life. This means that most modern-day Pagans have to come to their religion on their own. People turn to Paganism for many reasons. Many feel a calling to the beauty and mystery of Earth and nature and experience those things as sacred before they even know there are Earth-based religions. To them, the cycles of the days, the seasons, and the many changes in life are sacred and more than just interesting footnotes in the time between birth and death. Pagans are often avid readers and love exploring theology, philosophy, psychology, and the occult but are also willing to express religious feelings through the body, heart, and soul. Some come seeking a balance of energies that they feel are lacking in the world. Religion and culture have been historically patriarchal and the worship and adoration of the sacred feminine (the Goddess) is a way to balance that uneven influence of the masculine. Others have become increasingly alarmed at the degree of environmental degradation that humans have inflicted on Earth. They see the problem not just as a social challenge but as a moral obligation. They believe that the solution to the crisis, the only way we can save our selves and the planet, is to approach it through a spiritual awareness. There are those who are attracted to the personal and religious freedom offered through this alternative theology. These and many other factors are reasons that people find themselves drawn to Paganism. I have heard many people exclaim that finding Paganism felt like coming home.

What Pagans Do Not Do

One of things I want to do with this book is to dispel some of the common misconceptions that abound about Paganism. Some of the confusion comes from the use of the word Pagan to represent a new religion (though based on some ancient concepts). One of the origins of the word represented those who lived in the countryside of the Rome. Once Christianity became the official religion of the Roman Empire, it spread primarily through Rome and other major metropolitan areas. Conversion of the pagan people in the rural parts of the empire took much longer. The term went from signifying a country dweller to labeling the non-Christian as simpletons and ignorant folk. It began to have the same connotation that the word *redneck* has to us now.

Pagans do not worship the devil. Eventually being non-Christian also meant being in alliance with the devil. The term pagan began to take on the meaning of being one who worships the devil. That connection remains with us today even though the concept of the devil was a creation of Jewish and Christian theology. Pagans do not worship the devil. There are some who call themselves Satanists and there is an ongoing debate as to whether or not they should be called Pagans but even they will make a distinction between Satan and the devil. For Satanists, Satan is yet another possible god to honor like other Pagans honor the gods of specific pantheons. Modern Satanists may be more hedonistic in their practice than some other Pagans but their spiritual practice is not focused on doing evil.

Pagans do not sacrifice. It is true that a central focus to the practice of ancient pagans (and other religions such as Judaism) was to make sacrifices to the gods. These sacrifices included human and animal victims and it became one of the goals of the spreading influence of Christianity to stop this practice in any culture it encountered. For a vast majority of people, these practices are now seen as cruel and that includes modern Pagans. The moral code of not causing harm and the concept that all beings are sacred means that today's Pagans have no need or desire to engage in any kind of living sacrifice. The purpose of the ancient practice of sacrifice was to appease the gods by giving something valuable to them that would convince them to provide a bountiful harvest for the community. Developing agricultural societies soon realized that they could not eat all the vegetables and fruit they sowed from a harvest or there would be nothing left. Instead of eating everything that Earth provided, they knew that they would have to put aside some of that precious food for future needs. If they harvested corn, for example, they would have received the corn from Earth but would also have had to return some of that corn back to Earth so that she would provide it again for the next year. Some of the corn had to be sacrificed back to the provider. Some cultures then extended the same principle to the growth of their livestock and to their children. Long before the advent of veterinary science and pediatric medicine, the birth rate for animals and children could sometimes be frustratingly low. To compensate for this reality, those early societies thought that they could return an animal or a young member of their community back to the gods thus making it possible for more to be made available in the future. Modern Pagans can maintain the lessons of sacrifice without actually exercising any harmful actions. We can learn to sacrifice some of the things that are important to us such as our time, energy, and money to our communities in order to contribute to the overall health of the society.

Similar to the concept of Karma, many Pagans believe that when we commit ourselves to doing helpful things for ourselves, for others, and for the world, that we, in return, are enriched. Some see it as a matter of sending positive energy into the world that is then returned back to the sender. Some say that the energy is actually returned threefold. Since, according to the laws of physics, energy can neither be created or destroyed, how can it be magnified three times in return? Actually, it is not magnified; the energy you send out is simply reverberated in several places. When a sound is sent into a room, its energy is reflected by the surfaces within the room and some of those surfaces actually begin to vibrate (it is called sympathetic vibration) and send additional sounds into the space. The same is true for our personal energy. When we send out energy in the form of thoughts, actions, words, physical movements, feelings, or expressions, that energy is reflected in at least three places. It is reflected within ourselves, within our environment, and through the people and beings around us. Each of those places reflect and vibrate with that energy and then return sympathetic vibrations. Doing positive things and sending out compassionate energy can be way of offering sacrifice to the universe so that good can be returned.

Pagans do not worship idols. Although it is common to see sacred altars with religious images and symbols in the homes of many Pagans, it is a mistake to assume that the objects on the altar are the actual focus of the worship. Worshipping an idol means that some image or object is treated as if it were the deity itself. For example, a statue of Shiva would not represent Shiva, it would actually *be* Shiva. Though everything may be considered a part of divinity no one object can be the totality of divinity. Any symbols, idols, images, or statues on an altar are there to remind the practitioner of divine ideas and principles. Those things are only tools and symbols and are meant to represent deeper truths and things that may be difficult to simply put into words.

Pagans do not believe in sin. Most Pagans do not believe in the concept that we should be ashamed of our bodies. For many, the body is to be celebrated and the pleasures of touch and sensation are not seen as distractions to the religious quest but are part of the total experience of spiritual living. The mind, heart, body, and soul are equally part of who we are and each can make possible access to the divine since each is part of the divine. Sexuality, compassion, contemplation, and artistic expression can all be part of a deep holistic spiritual practice or set of practices. The idea that we are born sinful creatures who must spend our lives seeking redemption is foreign to most Pagans. We are born equally as sparks of the divine. We are born neither evil nor good, just sacred. Evil and good are seen as consequences of the decisions made by humans and the actions ensued from those decisions. Everything begins with intent. Pagans strive to have a clear intent about everything they do especially in religious matters and practices. Those who consciously intend to do harm and then choose to act upon that intent by actually causing harm may be said to commit evil acts. Nature knows not evil nor good; it knows only cycles of change and balance. Earth has no intent to harm when a hurricane appears, for example. Hurricanes exist because they are one way that oceans cool off as a part of the planet moves into Winter. The fact that some are harmed or hurt in the wake of a hurricane does not make it evil because there was no conscious intent to harm behind the action.

What Pagans Do

Now that we have seen what it is that Pagans do not do, we will look at some practices that are uniquely Pagan. What is important to remember is that there is no central creed or directive that requires that all Pagans do the same kind of practices. Each person is free to do as little or as much as he or she likes. The only thing that matters is that each person find a way to connect to his or her idea of the divine through practices that connect to the mind, heart, body, and soul.

Some Pagans practice magick but you do not have to practice magick to be a Pagan. I define magick as any act of conscious transformation. Again, intent is important. Not all things can be transformed at will regardless of how many fancy words, ornate tools, or wild gestures you may use. We all exist within the material world of Earth and cannot go against the universal laws of physics. Despite the claims of the titles of many books on spell craft, you cannot get a lover to show up at your door by just lighting a candle, but there is one thing that you can transform much easier - yourself. You can make a conscious effort to become the person with the positive frame of mind that better attracts a lover. Magick, when done as a spiritual practice, can be a form of active prayer. It is active because you are combining your personal energy with the energy that permeates the universe in order to fulfill a need or desire as defined by your intent.

Some Pagans practice in groups but you do not have to be in a group to be a Pagan. There are a variety of Pagan groups in every major metropolitan area (and beyond) throughout the U.S. and in other countries as well. Those groups can be closed (by invitation only) such as covens and magickal groups. Others are public groups such as those that celebrate the Sabbats through public ritual. There are also public Pagan classes, festivals, and workshops. There are large and small learning and study groups and there are many online covens, groups, schools, and discussion rooms. Unlike the traditional religions, however, regular participation in group spiritual practices is not required. There are many Pagans who prefer to practice alone. Pagans are free to do spiritual practices in groups or as individuals.

Some Pagans wear ritual clothes or are naked during rituals but you do not have to wear fancy robes or remove your clothing to be a Pagan. There are those Pagans who are into getting fancy ritual tools and wearing ornate robes and clothing but these things are not essential to any spiritual practice. Some wear fancy clothes to represent to themselves and others that a ritual is meant to be something different than what is done in the mundane day-to-day world. Ritual and spiritual practices are meant to transport the individual beyond the needs of the ego and connect him or her to the divine. Creating a sacred space and wearing ritual clothes can be a way to denote that difference. Of course, some Pagans wear fancy clothes just because it is fun. It is no coincidence that Pagans tend to be attracted to Renaissance fairs and period costume events. Some Pagans practice their rituals in the nude for similar reasons that some prefer to wear robes. Being nude reminds us that we are not doing what is routine in the mundane world and doing a ritual without clothing is, for some, a way to be united with the truly natural self and the naked world. As I mentioned above, the body is meant to be appreciated for its inherent beauty; it is not a source of shame or guilt. We can best come to understand this when we become naked and embrace our own natural beauty - especially when we are in the midst of sacred space and spiritual intent.

Some Pagans wear a pentagram but you do not need to don any special jewelry to be a Pagan. For some Pagans, the five pointed star in a circle represents the essence of Pagan teaching. Its five points are said to symbolize the four classical elements: Earth, Air, Fire, and Water along with the quintessential element - Spirit. The star is usually situated with one tip pointed upwards to denote that Spirit is above the other elements. The star itself is a symbol of hope and of light in the darkness. It also represents humanity (think DaVinci's "Vitruvian Man") and symbolizes that we are equally part of the divine and are not separate from it. The Pentagram is also said to symbolize the planet Venus because the planet ascribes a pentagram shape to observers on Earth. The planet Venus, of course, is named after a female Greek goddess and, thus, represents the feminine aspect. The Pentagram, then, helps to remind us that feminine forces are an essential part of the energy of the universe and that men and women are truly equal in the unity of Spirit.

Some Pagans believe in gods and goddesses but you do not have to believe in any deities to be Pagan. There are Pagans who honor a pantheon of gods and goddesses such as those of the Roman, Greek, or Egyptian pantheons. There are those who worship only one deity they call the Goddess and there are others who worship no gods at all. For some Pagans the ultimate reality is the energy of the universe, Spirit, or nature itself. All that matters is the recognition of a sacredness to all beings and all things regardless of how that sacredness is specifically experienced. The fact that there are so many different opinions about the divine among Pagans is not a bad thing. Rather, it is one of the strengths of Paganism and one of the reasons that many people are attracted to it. Personal practices will also differ to reflect the individual's understanding and relationship to the divine. This, too, is a good thing for people do not necessarily need to worship in the same way in order to act as a group confirmation of beliefs.

Some Pagans engage in elaborate rituals individually or in groups but you do not have to do any fancy rituals to be a Pagan. As we have already seen, an individual's practice in Paganism can be as simple or as complex as he or she desires and can be done privately or in groups but no specific type of practice is required of any Pagan. All that matters is that, within your mind, you possess an understanding of the sacredness of all things and that within your heart is a feeling that you are, indeed, connected to that universal divinity. How you choose to express or affirm that in your daily life is up to you but, in the very least, the decisions you make on how to live your life and interact with others and Earth should be informed and inspired by your Pagan beliefs and understanding of the universe.

Some Pagans practice various forms of divination but you do not have to do any sort of divination in order to be a Pagan. The word divination often brings up all sorts of images of strangely dressed people flipping worn and mysterious cards while doling out dire predictions about the future. Although there are some who desire to maintain that image of power and mystery, the reality about divination is really quite different. Nowadays, many people use varied tools of divination (such as rune stones, tarot cards, or I-Ching coins, to name a few) to help themselves or others find ways to solve problems or see challenges in a unique way. All divination systems depend on symbols to help the seeker reach into the unconscious mind to seek new visions or ideas. Through these symbols, people can gain new insights into particular situations or difficulties. Divination tools are just that - tools. People of all religions seek answers to their questions through their leaders or through various tools such as sacred texts or religious practices. Divination can be a spiritual practice as well but, like many other Pagan practices, it is more interactive. Through divinatory symbols, one can feel more connected to the deep mysteries of the universe and to the divine by relating to the personal and collective unconscious.

Some Pagans engage in energy work but you do not have to manipulate energies to be a Pagan. Some Pagans see the universe as all connected through a single collective of energy that vibrates at different states to give us the myriad of things that we experience. Since all living things are equally endowed with this energy, some believe that we can manipulate those personal energies and influence the energy around us as well. For some, this is the essence of magick but it can also be the basis for spiritual or energy healing in which energy is transfered to those who need it for healing. Other religious traditions might call it the power of prayer but, instead of asking the divine for this energy, Pagans who do energy work see themselves as a conduit of healing energy. Such energy manipulation can also be done by the self to promote strong energy flow and self health.

All in all, you do not have to do anything to be a Pagan. Paganism is, ultimately, a way of seeing and living in the world. If you accept the Three Pillars then you can just *be* Pagan in your heart and live it through your daily actions. If you honor all things as sacred, are true to your intent, are responsible for your decisions, and like to observe and honor the changes in life and the cycles in the universe, then your own personal Paganism will be reflected in your life. Of course, you can also study and engage in any other Pagan spiritual practice you choose and you can join in any number of Pagan groups and gatherings you desire, but none of these things is required for you to be a Pagan.

A Religion for the 21st Century

Chapter Four

Simple Pagan Practices

"One can have the clearest and most complete knowledge of what is and yet not be able to deduct from that what should be the goal of our human aspirations" ~ *Einstein*

If you have come this far in my book then you may be someone (like many others before you) who feels that Paganism is the right theology for you and for our time. If so, I want to introduce some very simple practices that can be done to help you celebrate your Pagan views. There are, of course, many great texts out there that explain many different types of Pagan practices. Those practices can range from the very simple to the very complex but I want to introduce here some practices that are very easy to incorporate into the busy lifestyle that many of us lead. Spiritual practices do not have to be complex nor do they have to be done in a particular space or lead by a particular leader. A spiritual practice can be anything that helps you create and maintain a relationship with things greater than the self; they can be done anywhere and at anytime. They can be done in groups or by one's self but the activity is not as important as is the attitude and the experience of the person engaged in the activity. For something to be a Pagan spiritual practice, it should help one relate to the universal divine. Since I claim that the Three Pillars are the essence of Pagan theology then Pagan practices need to reflect those principles.

Practices for the First Pillar

One of the first Pagan practices you might do is to contemplate upon what you feel is the ultimate reality of the universe. The first Pillar claims that all things are sacred but does not define what the "what" is that unites and relates all things. How can there be both separateness and unity? What is the common element within all things? How does it become manifest to become the world as we experience it? You are free and encouraged to determine the answers to these questions (and others) on your own. Once you have such an understanding, then you should look to see how this reality is evident in the world and in your life. What would it be like to live in a world where everything is truly sacred?

Through the first Pillar, nature and mankind are regarded as equally sacred and part of the same divine wholeness. One way to experience this universal relationship to nature is to simply spend as much time out-of-doors. Hiking, camping, and walking in the woods or other open spaces can help you connect with Earth and all her plant and animal children. Stargazing and night time walks can help you relate to the great expanse of the universe.

Paganism seeks to be a holistic religion. All parts of the self are considered equally divine. This includes the body. The body should be celebrated and appreciated regardless of its shape, size, or color. Learn to experience the world through your senses. Literally, smell the roses along the path. Be conscious of the taste of the foods and drinks you consume, the things that your fingers touch, the aromas that your nose encounters, and the music and sounds that you hear. Revel in the pleasure of responsible sexuality - for the same creative energy that brought about the universe is part of the process of bringing about a new child into the world. If the universe can practice creation without shame why should not we be able to do the same? Feed the mind, tantalize the body, feel all the emotions that your heart encounters in life and you will enrich your soul. In short, learn to live, love, and laugh.

Another easy spiritual practice is to wear a pendant with a symbol that represents your beliefs and what is important to you. Some wear a pentagram either over or under their clothing. Whatever you wear should reflect your feelings and you should take some time to contemplate the symbolism of the objects within the pendant. With a pentagram, everything has meaning: the circle around it, the star, the five points, the orientation of the star, the shape of the star, etc. All of these things should reflect your understanding of the universe.

Practices for the Second Pillar

The Second Pillar is about the choices we make in life. Pagans are free to choose their spiritual and life practices as they see fit. But, with those choices comes the responsibility of being accountable for the actions made as a result of those choices. A simple Pagan practice based on the Second Pillar is to consider carefully your true intent for each action. Be honest with yourself and others about your intent and follow it carefully as you act upon your decisions. Consider adopting the policy of seeking to avoid harm to all beings whenever possible. Consider your intent in terms of this or any other ethical principles you may have determined for yourself. Think not just about your decisions to act but upon the possible consequences to all involved if you go through with your action. Be responsible. Do not agree to do anything you cannot do reasonably and within your own principles. If you say you will do something then you should do your best to follow through with your promise. Some Pagans light a candle of intent before every ritual. This candle serves to remind the practitioner of the intent of the ritual throughout. Every other candle on the altar is lit with this one candle so that the intent is symbolically spread into every corner of the sacred space. You can light a single candle at times when you want to remind yourself of your intent. I often light a candle before making dinner to remind me of my intent to create a delicious and nutritious meal filled with love for my family.

Your intent should be clear in everything you do - at home, at work, and in your relationships with others. Sometimes it is not possible or appropriate to light a candle. Any object can serve as a reminder of your intent. I keep a small green stone on my desk at work to remind me of my intent to teach with compassion and to maintain high standards in my classes. Stones, amulets, jewelry, fragrances from incense, symbols, statues, posters and placards, or any other object can serve to keep you focused on the intent you have chosen. In some situations, you can create a candle-like hand position by interlacing your fingers and letting your index fingers point out together to serve as a reminder of your intent or of your ideals.

A good way to set your intent for living a Pagan spiritual life is to create a spiritual vow such as the one below which can be based on your theological principles. The vow should reflect your beliefs and serve as a reminder to you as to how you plan to live out those values in your daily life.

> ### My Personal Vow
>
> Through Reason, Respect, Responsibility, Reverence, and Revelry
> do I vow to live in Spirit.

You can also combine your vow with your pendant practice. When you put on your pendant in the morning you can repeat your vow or affirmation allowing your pendant to remind you of that vow throughout the day. When you remove the pendant before going to bed you can take a moment to recall your day and think about how well you lived up to your vow. If you think you fell short of your personal goal then do not be harsh on yourself. Just consider what you can do next time to be more in align with your intent.

Practices for the Third Pillar

The third Pillar is about honoring the many continuous cycles that make up our world and our lives. There are cosmic cycles, there are life cycles, and there are cycles of energy that influence who we are and the people with whom we interact. As Pagans we take time to honor those changes within our lives. Birthdays are a good opportunity to celebrate and honor the changes that take place throughout a life cycle. We go through many stages of development in our lives. Each one has its particular challenges and opportunities. Recognizing those opportunities and taking advantage of them is one way to enjoy what life has to offer. Our youth-centered culture has made us afraid of birthdays but we can make them a time to reflect upon and appreciate the particular joys of each age. A candle on a birthday cake can be a candle of intent offering you an opportunity to consider what you plan to do in the coming year. Some ancient Greeks and Romans believed that everyone had a guardian spirit and that entity was honored on a person's birthday. Gifts were often brought to royalty on their birthdays. Certainly you deserve to be a king or queen for a day!

Another way to celebrate and honor cycles is to maintain a careful balance of energies within ourselves. We need to be active and engaged in life but we also need to rest and reflect. Become active in life by engaging in creative, expressive, and challenging activities but also learn to appreciate the down times as well. Sports, the arts, hobbies, learning about new things, and interacting positively with others are just some of the many ways in which people can become engaged in life. Spiritual pursuits such as taking part in rituals, engaging in prayer or magick, helping others, studying sacred works, taking classes, and attending Pagan events can help you develop your own active practice. Those things all need to be balanced, however, with passive practices that allow you to rest and reflect. Meditation is an excellent means of providing balance to a busy life. Other simple practices can include taking the time to enjoy a lazy day outside in nature, making time to take short naps, learning to stretch and breathe in order to relax throughout the day, and finding ways to take energy restoring breaks.

Many Pagans honor the changing cycle of the seasons by recognizing eight days of the year as special. These days are called Sabbats and are celebrated on the two solstices, the two equinoxes, and eight days in between those dates. For each one, you can take time to recognize the change in the season and find a simple practice to honor the day. My discussion below will deal with the Sabbats that are experienced in the the Northern Hemisphere but people in the Southern Hemisphere can adjust accordingly.

The Pagan Sabbats (Northern Hemisphere)			
Name	Approximate Date	Event	Season
Samhain	November 1		Height of Fall
Yule	December 21	Winter Solstice	Start of Winter
Imbolc	February 1		Height of Winter
Ostara	March 21	Spring Equinox	Start of Spring
Beltane	May 1		Height of Spring
Litha	June 21	Summer Solstice	Start of Summer
Lammas	August 1		Height of Summer
Mabon	September 21	Fall Equinox	Start of Fall

Samhain is a good time to honor your ancestors. The secular traditions of Halloween come from some pagan practices in which it was believed that the spirits of the dead were able to return to the world of the living. The traditional activities of wearing costumes and carving pumpkins helps us to honor the darker side of life and can be an opportunity to pay respect to those loved ones that have passed away.

The season of Yule also maintains many enjoyable and ancient pagan practices. Bringing an evergreen into the house in the midst of Winter was a way of honoring one of the few trees that seems to still be alive during the dead cold months. People used to believe that the presence of such a tree in the house would help keep the inhabitants alive as well. The burning of the Yule log helps to signify the sun whose light will begin to fade after this time. In our house, we often celebrate the 12 days of Yule. Each day represents the sun rising in each of the coming 12 months and we reflect upon our hopes for the coming year. Keeping the fire of the Yule log burning helps to keep warmth in the house and to look forward to the time when the sun's warmth will return. Since Yule is the Winter Solstice, I often get up very early, brave the cold, and find a place to watch the sun rise because the solstice dawn is the birth of a new sun.

In the cold Northeast, the Sabbat of Imbolc is truly a special occasion because it signals that Winter is at its midpoint. This is a period of great darkness and cold so any amount of hope for the arrival of the Spring is welcome. In our house, we often celebrate

Imbolc by turning off all unnecessary electric and electronic components and fill the house only with the light of candles. Doing so makes us acutely aware of the dark and the image of flickering candles all through the house provides a special romantic kind of light and warmth that light bulbs and flickering television screens cannot. Imbolc is the time when some animals begin to produce milk for their future offspring. We can honor this by drinking a milk or milk substitute beverage. The drink can be as simple as a glass of milk (or soy milk) or as fancy as a special shake or float.

Ostara is the beginning of Spring when many different varieties of animals prepare to produce their offspring. Symbols of new birth abound during this time. The egg and the rabbit have always symbolized fertility which was particularly important to ancient cultures who had to contend with consistent low birth rates and high levels of infant mortality. The ancient Pagan practice of coloring and decorating eggs is still with us today and is a fun way to celebrate Ostara. This is also a good time to think about the upcoming planting season. You can get some seeds from a store or from your own plant collection and offer them a blessing for good growth then save the seeds in a special place until it is time to plant them. Ostara is the beginning of the bright half of the year when the sun's light is longer in the day than the darkness of night. It is at this time we switch from drinking wine with meals to drinking beer and I will often honor that first glass of beer.

Beltane has traditionally been the season of fun and frolic. It is the season of the May Day. In earlier times, the phrase "going a Maying" meant it was time to run and dance in the long tall grass and that it was time to run and catch a mate. Beltane is the time when many animals begin producing offspring while food is readily available and the coming Summer provides a chance for raising the young. It is a time to honor the body and the wonders of our sexuality. Beltane can be the time to start or renew a romantic relationship. In a sense, Beltane is the Pagan version of Valentine's Day but with less inhibition. The tradition of decorating and dancing around the Maypole was a way of honoring sexuality through a phallic symbol but celebrating with May poles usually takes a coordinated effort. A simpler way to practice Beltane is decorate a tree with colorful ribbons. The family can also be brought together to play active or board games.

Litha is the celebration of the Summer Solstice. It is the day where the light of the sun is celebrated because days will become shorter (in terms of light) after this day. I often watch the sunset on this day and feel kind of melancholic about the upcoming loss of light even though I know that there are still many warm days ahead. Litha is a day when we should honor rest and its importance in our lives. I think it would be great if everybody had this day off and we all promised to do nothing except rest and relax with each other. If it all possible, celebrate Litha by finding a comfortable place to just lie around and do nothing. In our busy lives, doing nothing for a whole day is a radical concept.

Lammas is the Sabbat at the height of summer and is traditionally the time of the great harvest. This is the day that should be all about food. We often have a big dinner such as a fancy fondue meal with appetizers, main entrees, and desserts. Usually the meal is comprised of local foods that are in season.

Mabon is the Spring Equinox. This is a time to enjoy the changing colors of the leaves and to prepare for the coming Winter. We often enjoy taking a ride or a hike to look at the changing colors of the leaves here in the Northeast. It is also the beginning of the darker time of the year and we honor that by switching from drinking beer with meals to drinking wine. Mabon is the time to honor the first glass of wine.

Postlude

"The single greatest world transformation would simply be the embrace of global reasonableness and pluralistic tolerance" ~ *Wilber*

Religion has long been a source of great comfort and of great strife in the world. Many wars and crimes against humanity have been the result of religious intolerance. Democracies are supposed to embrace the concept of the separation of church and state as our the Founding Fathers of the United States sought to do when they wrote the Bill of Rights. That separation is constantly being threatened because some do not subscribe to the wisdom of that philosophy. It is interesting to note that, at the time when the U.S. was coming together as a new nation, the religious fundamentalists were some of the strongest and most vocal supporters of the separation of church and state. The reason is that the dominant religion at the time was the Church of England or the Anglican church and it was those churches that would have been given state support and influence upon the government. Christian fundamentalists wanted to be free to roam the country and spread their own version of Christianity and, so, fought against state support of religion. Nowadays, however, the situation has been reversed as religious fundamentalism seeks to control political power at all levels. Even though the U.S. Constitution was ratified in the18th Century and many other emerging democracies adopted similar principles in their constitutions, the battle to establish control of democratic governments and to gain power through conversion by religious institutions continues. But, it does not have to be this way.

I believe that as humanity continues to grow and develop, its overall consciousness slowly continues to awaken. We are just beginning to understand how truly globally connected we are to one another and to the planet and the environment in which we live. We are slowly realizing that what we do affects others and the world as a whole. The recent world financial situation shows us that economies of all the nations of the world are intertwined and not independent. We are slowly awakening from the dream-land concept that said that we could do whatever we wanted to ourselves, to each other, and to the environment without suffering the consequences of those actions. We are beginning to grasp the idea that the universe is alive and is infinitely more mysterious and awesome than we may ever be able to comprehend and we have come to know that we do not have to understand it all. We are learning that not everything is not clearly *this* or *that* nor is everything chartable on a straight line. Our consciousness struggles to come to terms with the realities of the 21st Century but our religious traditions do not.

Much to the chagrin of many contemporary philosophers, religion has not gone away. In fact, it has become an even more dominant part of our cultural identity and many current religions have not shown a willingness to change to suit the needs of the Postmodern world. Instead of hoping and dreaming that something will change on its own, it is time to seek the change needed by developing and nurturing new religions that support current realities such as personal exploration, religious and cultural tolerance, personal responsibility, interconnectedness, a respect for the feminine, and a holistic understanding of the self. Paganism is one such religion. It is a Postmodern religion that deserves to be understood and respected as well as any other religion.

Being Pagan is both simple and complex. Since there is no formal method of conversion, anyone can become Pagan at any time yet being truly Pagan can be a challenge. It is not easy to see all things as sacred in a world that still considers nature a vast wasteland and development opportunity and people as just opportunities for exploitation. Living in a way that encourages sustaining Earth and all her children will require acting and thinking in a different way than has been done before. We do not have to all live in log cabins but we do have to consider how to renew, recycle, and reuse and we have to find ways to harness and use energy in a way that does not destroy the planet and ourselves. Yet, this may be the only way to survive. We can make it happen when we realize the importance to our own survival.

Making this realization a spiritual truth may be an important first step. Being Pagan means seeing the world as alive and sacred. It means seeing all people asa part of the divine – and that includes the guy that just cut you off on the freeway. It means considering the intent of all your actions and taking responsibility for the results of those actions. It means honoring the constant cycles of life and the universe. It means being the truly natural person that you were born to be.

Appendix

Bibliography

Adler, Margaret. *Drawing Down The Moon.* 1986, Penguin Books.

Angell, David J.R., Justyn D. Comer, and Mathew L.N. Wilkinson. *Sustaining Earth: Response to the Environmental Threats.* 1991, St. Martin's Press.

Berger, Peter L. *The Sacred Canopy: Elements of a Sociological Theory of Religion.* 1967, Doubleday and Co.

Braun, Willi and Russell T. McCutcheon, eds. *Guide to the Study of Religion.* 2000, Cassell.

Butler, Christopher. *Postmodernism: A Very Short Introduction.* 2002, Oxford University Press.

Crosby, Donald A. *A Religion of Nature.* 2002, State University of New York Press.

Dukas, Helen and Banesh Hoffman, ed. *Albert Einstin - The Human Side.* 1979, Princeton Univ Press.

Eilers, Dana D. *The Practical Pagan.* 2002, New Page Books.

Goswami, Amit. *The Visionary Window: A Quantum Physicist's Guide to Enlightenment.* 2000, Theosophical Publishing House.

Green, William Scott and Jacob Neusner, ed. *The Religion Factor: An Introduction to How Religion Matters.* 1996, Westminster John Knox Press.

Grenz, Stanley. *A Primer on Postmodernism. 1996, Wm. B. Eerdmans Publishing Co.*

Heelas, Paul and Linda Woodhead. *Why Religion Is Giving Way to Spirituality.* 2005, Blackwell Publishing.

Herbert, David. *Religion and Civil Society: Rethinking Public Religion in the Contemporary World.* 2003, Ashgate Publishing Co.

Higginbotham, Joyce and River. *Paganism: An Introduction to Earth-Centered Religions.* 2002, Llewellyn.

Huxley, Aldous. *The Perennial Philosophy.* 1945, Harper and Row.

Jammer, Max. *Einstein and Religion.* 1997, Princeton University Press.

Lovelock, James. *Gaia: The Practical Science of Planetary Science.* 2000, Gaia Books Limited.

Magee, John B. *A Study of the Religious Meaning of Being Human.* 1967, Harper and Row.

Pearce, Jospeh Chilton. *The Death of Religion and the Rebirth of Spirit: A Return to the Intelligence of the Heart.* 2007, Park Street Press.

Sheldrake, Rupert. *The Rebirth of Nature: The Greening of Science and God.* 1991, Bantam Books.

Smith, Huston. *The World's Religions.* 1991, Harper Collins.

Talbot, Michael. *Mysticism and the New Physics.* 1993, Penguin.

Tillich, Paul. *Theology of Culture.* 1959, Oxford University Press.

Underhill, Evelyn. *Mysticism: The Nature and Development of Spiritual Consciousness.* 2002, Dover Publications.

Ward, Keith. *The Case For Religion.* 2004, OneWorld Publications.

Wilber, Ken. *A Theory of Everything.* 2001, Shambhala.

Wilber, Ken. *Sex, Ecology, Spirituality: The Spirit of Evolution.* 2000, Shambhala.

York, Michael. *Pagan Theology.* 2003, New York University Press.

About the Author

Shanddaramon is a published writer, composer, and poet and is the author of several books and articles on living and being a modern Pagan. He lives in the Boston, Massachusetts, area with his wife, daughter, dog, and 2 cats. When not writing, he is a Professor of Music and teaches classes at a local college. He has often sought ways in which to combine his interest in the arts with a growing interest in the mystical and, specifically, through Paganism. He applies these skills through his art and writing and through services such as divinatory advising, pastoral counseling and ritual work. Combining the arts with mysticism, he has created classes and workshops for others with similar interests and has led rituals for organizations and individuals.

A Religion for the 21ˢᵗ Century

Other Books
by Shanddaramon

For Adults:

1. *Self Initiation for the Solitary Witch: Attaining Higher Spirituality Through a Five Degree System.* New Page Books, 2004.
2. *Living Paganism: An Advanced Guide for the Solitary Practitioner.* New Page Books, 2005.
3. *Dewdrops In The Moonlight: A Book of Pagan Prayer.* Astor Press, 2007.
4. *The Sacred Quest: A Pagan Perspective on the Pursuit of Happiness.* Astor Press, 2008.
5. *The Worlds of Tarot: Expanding the Tarot Universe.* Astor Press, 2009.

For Children:

1. *Sabbats of the Northern Hemisphere: A Pagan Book for Children.* Astor Press, 2008.
2. *The Twelve Days of Yule: A Pagan Children's Activity Book.* Astor Press, 2009.

www.ingramcontent.com/pod-product-compliance
Lightning Source LLC
Chambersburg PA
CBHW031330040426
42443CB00005B/281